To Diane
Enjoy!
CP Taylor

The Island of Lost Jobs

A collection of short stories
about employment

by E. P. Taylor

These stories are based on real experiences
but most of the names and places have been
altered to protect the privacy of the
participants.

Acknowledgements

Many thanks to our public library for hosting the Adult Writing Group, and to our Adult Writing Group for all its help, encouragement and camaraderie.

Dedication

To my daughter Hannah, who is entering the
workforce, and to my husband Ken, who is
looking forward to
retirement.

Introduction

There are a number of littler jobs I haven't included here because they lasted a day or less and could not fill a whole chapter. Like the time I took a job as a waitress at a run-down German restaurant. The uniform was a little peasant fräulein costume with a draw-string top, laced bodice, dirndl skirt and apron. I was in my early twenties and didn't look half bad in it. Apparently the only customers I had all afternoon thought so, too. For two hours, four old drunk guys in suits sat in the only occupied (German?) table in the dimly lit dining room, drank martinis, smoked cigars, laughed and tugged on my costume. Then they disappeared, leaving me fifteen cents for a tip. Presumably I might have made more if I had sat on their laps or something. I decided I didn't need to find out about that. At the end of my shift I hung the costume up in the ladies room and never returned. Not much of a story, but I suppose I learned about what I would tolerate to make a buck. Or in this case, fifteen cents. So, like every job, it was valuable as a learning experience.

As a freelance artist, I have had been lucky enough to be able to work at things I loved to do whenever possible. In between those times, I have also had the privilege to gain life experiences through short term employment. Looking back now, I can appreciate,

and even relish, the absurdity of some of
these situations

I got my first few jobs as a teenager, and
even those short-lived experiences seem to
have shaped me more than I realized at the
time. My hope is that all those who have ever
lost a job will be able to recognize themselves somewhere in these pages and enjoy a
well-earned laugh.

Table of Contents

The Island of Lost Jobs

Chapter One

COUNTER WORK

It was my friend Joanne who suggested that we try to get a job at Dino's Hamburgers. Sweet, quiet, unassuming Joanne. I had met her on our first day of high school, in art class. She had seemed almost unbearably shy and awkward at first. When she spoke I could hardly hear her. It's a good thing I was intimidated by the older students in the class or I might never have tuned onto her frequency. As it was, we were the only two sophomores at a table of junior-year art students and we were both fairly petrified. I mean, there we were, only freshly turned fifteen, exposed to these sophisticated, worldly people of sixteen. We were mortified. Gradually though, Joanne became used to my presence and I began to notice the humorously subversive remarks that she uttered under her breath. It turned out that she was very funny and I grew to enjoy her company. Over time I learned that she came from a broken home, as did I. We became best friends.

Little pencil-thin, midwestern, soft-spoken, moon-faced Joanne was also an instigator, and I very much admired that side of her, even if it got us both into heaps of trouble. Or maybe because of it. Joanne had a way of explaining what a waste of time it was, in the great scheme of things, to go to Biology class for instance. Why did we need to go and dissect earthworms, for heaven's sake, when we could sit under a stairwell and write free-verse poetry? Earthworm guts had all been seen before, but poetry- it was a noble excursion into the great creative unknown. Who could argue with priorities like these? So Biology class was neglected in favor of sneaking off to our own productive writing wonderland, a secret place under the library stairwell, where someone had written "PEEEEEEEE-NEEEEEEE" on the underside of the metal stairs in black magic marker. Ah, to think of all the masterpieces we developed there. So many, in fact, that eventually we were sent to the girl's dean, (the formidable Mrs. Frawley who was notorious for making girls cry), who asked us why we were skipping class. Having no answer for her I checked my shoes for scuffs, but Joanne's tiny voice suddenly piped up with "Well, at the time it seemed the thing to do." How I admired Joanne for that answer! Mrs. Frawley simply did not know what to make of such frankness. She sent home notes and we promised not to do it again, but following a short grace period, of course we did. I have no idea how we graduated. Truancy was largely ignored back in those days, unless you went out and robbed convenience stores or something when you should have been in class. Nowadays schools are much more strict. Plus, we had a habit of getting very good grades in the classes we attended, like art and creative writing. We weren't slackers, we were just choosy about how we spent our time. It was pretty obvious (to us, at least) that we were not destined for the sciences.

With careers in biology now out of the question and our broken homes unable to throw money at us, it became clear that we would need to find jobs in order to afford a car to drive us to wherever a living might be made in creative writing. Thus Joanne decided that we should apply to a local burger chain called Dino's where she had seen a help wanted sign. Dino's was just a few blocks from school, so we could conveniently walk there after classes (or writing sessions) were done for the day. We went together to fill out the application forms, which seemed annoyingly long and complicated for a job that paid just $1.60 per hour. We had no work experience. We didn't even know our Social Security numbers, and had to take the forms home to complete them. We also had to get work permits, since we were under the legal employment age at the time. All the same, we wound up being hired.

The first thing we had to do, before we could actually start working the counter at the burger joint, was go through a week's worth of training. This consisted of going up into the attic of the Dino's building (who knew it had an attic?) and howling with ridicule at the preposterous slide show we had to watch in one hour increments without supervision by the manager, who was much too busy to tend to us. The presentation was all about how we needed to leave our own personalities behind and become part of the Dino's team. It explained how we were to wear our hair, how we needed to wash our hands, and how we needed to greet even the nastiest customer with a big Dino's smile.

During that first exciting pre-work week we were also expected to select a used, red, polyester knit mini-dress uniform out of a disheveled pile that was crumpled into a cardboard box in the Dino's attic. We were expected to be responsible for this attire during our employment. We were also informed that we had to buy our own hair nets (hair nets?!), pantyhose and white leather shoes for the job, even though we hadn't yet seen a pay check. The footwear couldn't be cheap white tennis shoes either, oh no- that was specified in the slide show. They had to be nice, new, clean, white, leather nurse-type shoes. Holy cow. What to do? Well, Joanne had the answer. We'd beg some money from our Moms and buy some interesting 'New Age' type shoes that Joanne had noticed in a store window. These turned out to be Kalso Earth Shoes, which were ergonomically designed by a Danish woman to support feet in a natural way, based on how footprints look in the sand. In short, the heels were lower than the front part of the foot, and the toe area was spread out, creating a wide square front that looked quite a lot like a duck foot. Amazingly, Earth Shoes came in white, so as to provide natural comfort for any hippies in the health field. They were much more expensive than regular nurse shoes, but we thought it would be worth it. I don't know how we convinced our Moms to front the money for these outlandish looking shoes, but we did. When we showed up in our uniforms for our first day behind the counter, the manager just about blew his top, but there was nothing he could do because technically they were white leather shoes.

For four weeks we worked there, during which we alternated between evening dinner rushes, where everything somehow became mixed up and customers complained, and periods of light boredom, during which we were not allowed to relax, but had to look busy by pretending to mop the counter or wash the windows. Friends would come in to laugh at us and we would punish them by

giving them free refills on their milkshakes.
In no time at all Joanne and I were separated
so as not to influence each other and found
ourselves working on different shifts, which
was not what we'd had in mind.

Our first paychecks finally came after the
second two-week pay period, and after taxes
and shoe reimbursement we found that we
each had around eleven dollars left over, with
which to celebrate. Four weeks of work and
eleven dollars to show for it. I could feel my
work ethic sag at the knees just like the cheap
pantyhose I was wearing.

The very next week after that astounding
payday was a school holiday. I was in my
back yard reading a book while trying to get
some sun on my legs in an attempt to fake the
manager into thinking I was wearing stock-

ings. It was then that I made a subconscious decision not to check the time. I would just keep right on reading in the sun. I would postpone crawling into my deep-fried-patty-scented, red polyester knit mini dress, Earth Shoes and hair net, and then paying for the public transit bus to take me to work, where I would smile like a chimpanzee, pitch for the corporate team and generally whore myself for $1.60 an hour. No. Instead, I would just keep reading. So I did. I read and read. I also got more and more red as the early spring sun beat down on my skin, which had been larva-white after a long winter. I got a heck of a sunburn.

When I finally did show up for work, the boss was irate. Who could blame him? "I have a feeling you're not happy with your work," he blustered at me. How I wished I could be like Joanne and say "At the time it seemed the thing to do." Instead, I just murmured in agreement with him, saying that I was a vegetarian anyway, and probably should leave the job. Joanne was on duty, saw me leaving and thought that my face was red from being yelled at. It was just the sunburn.

Two weeks later I got my second and final paycheck for the second two-week period. It was sixty-two dollars, not big money but sixty-two dollars more than I had the day before, and I felt a pang of regret for not hanging in there to earn more. By that time Joanne had quit, too, simply explaining to the boss that she felt ill-suited. I wish I had been there to see that.

It wasn't a total loss, though. Those Earth Shoes were very well made and lasted for many years. In the punk rock 80's I used to paint mine with acrylic paints to suit my moods. So there was that. Too bad that the Kalso Earth Shoe store hadn't been hiring inexperienced fifteen year old girls to sell their shoes. There was a product I could have stood behind, my toes comfortably above my heels.

As for Joanne, she grew up, moved away, got married, got cancer and died a year after being diagnosed. I'm sure that wherever she is now, she is not regretting one moment spent writing free-verse poetry rather than going to class, or quitting any job that asked her not to be herself. For that matter, neither do I.

Chapter Two
HOSTESS

My first car was a used, 1968 Volkswagen Karmann Ghia. My father had bought it for me for $900.00 with the understanding that I was to pay it off in installments of $50.00. each month. It was a cute little yellow convertible. There were so many dimples under its fresh coat of yellow paint, that it was plain to see that much of its metal had been replaced with body putty by the time it fell into my eager, seventeen-year-old hands. It regularly pooped out, but it was easy to jump start simply by rolling it down a hill or shaking the tiny battery connectors in the rear-mounted engine. It was what we called a "rag" (as in ragged out), but it was my baby.

Like any baby though, my little lemon required fuel and upkeep, and that meant that I needed to find a job. I had seen a HELP WANTED sign at a local restaurant and decided to go and find out about it. I wanted to make a good impression, so I wore a nice pair of wool slacks, and a cashmere sweater I had borrowed from my sister without her permission.

Lems billed itself as a family restaurant, so I foresaw no problems with becoming employed there. In fact, the manager seemed surprisingly gracious and enthusiastic about my interview, and offered me a job on the spot. That was before he found out my age. It seems that one of the things that made Lems restaurants popular was that they sold frosty mugs of beer, and being under 18, I was not allowed to serve alcohol. Who knew? After a fair amount of stammering and a discussion with another manager, I was told that they had been toying with the idea of hiring a hostess for the dinner shift, and they thought they'd try me out in that role. I asked if I would need a uniform, but they said no, that I should just wear what I had on at the interview. Uh-oh, I thought. But at least I was employed again. Things were looking up for me and my car.

Now Lems was a pretty nice place, and certainly a step up from Dino's. Instead of ordering at a counter, people sat at tables and placed their orders with waitresses, who wore dark blue polyester uniforms with red and white checkered aprons that looked like tablecloths. Still, it wasn't quite classy enough, really, to merit a hostess, so I felt a little uneasy. The waitresses worked their tails off, while I stood at a little podium at the front and greeted people, showed them to their seats, got them extra tableware, catsup and high chairs, emptied ashtrays, and wiped up any unsightly smudges and spills that occurred. Minimum wage had skyrocketed to $2 per hour by then, and I felt rather guilty for getting the big bucks for so little actual toil. Luckily, the waitresses were sweet people who showed me no ill will, so I did all I could to lighten their load.

Every so often, the manager would appear from the back office and strut about briefly, striking studly poses in my line of vision, while gazing aloofly at the parking lot. I made sure that when he turned around, I was always busy wiping greasy thumbprints off the window, or scraping baby spittle from the carpet, until he disappeared back into his lair.

Each night, a bunch of guys would come in after work for some chow and beer. There were about six or eight of them, and judging by their dusty hair and work clothes, I guessed that they were in construction. On my first night, they breezed by my podium to what I came to understand was their usual table. This table was located conveniently at the intersection of where people came in, and the rest of the dining room, right where everyone had to pass by them. They were basically good customers, except for one guy who wore a wool cap and would become rather outspoken after a few frosty mugs of beer. Then he would start muttering comments about anyone who passed by, which was pretty much everyone, including me. Since I had to pass by him continually, to monitor the room for signs of minor distress,

I would regularly hear him mutter. I eventually got to the point where I could understand every word he said. His comments were not of a gentlemanly nature, to say the least, and I soon grew weary of them. So one night he made a comment about the ample contents of my borrowed cashmere sweater, and I very casually and quietly made a comment about the scant contents of his wool cap. I smiled sweetly, he looked surprised, his friends had a good laugh, and that took care of that.

However, the next day the manager called and let me know that the hostess experiment wasn't quite working. I was then offered the position of waitress for the breakfast shift on weekends. Apparently the previous breakfast waitress could no longer find the time. Realizing that I could just as easily have been fired, I accepted the offer. Great, I thought, no more obnoxious beer guys and now I could earn tips!

The head waitress got me geared up with a polyester uniform, and spent a quiet Saturday morning showing me the ropes. She was a nice person, a college student, who would have taken the breakfast shift herself, she told me, but she worked late both weekend nights and didn't want to burn the candle at both ends. I understood. She also explained to me that since waitresses get tips, they do not get minimum wage. Instead of the $2 per hour I was making as hostess, I would now be paid $1 per hour. So my new position would have me working eight hours per weekend and getting paid eight dollars a week by Lems. "Don't worry," she said, "the tips *should* make up for it." I replayed her statement in my mind. There was something about the way she said the word "should".

I showed up for work Sunday morning and greeted the South American cook, who was back in the kitchen nonchalantly smoking a cigarette. As I readied the tables for the throngs I noticed that no-one else had come in to work. I was the one and only waitress on duty. Sunday morning dragged by, a couple of small families came in for breakfast after church, and that was all. The majority of the shift I spent alone in the dining room, singing along with "The Girl From Ipanema" and other big Muzak hits being played over the sound system. I figured it was just a slow day. In a way, I was relieved because it was so easy, and because the weird manager wasn't there, but the tips I had hoped to earn were few and far between. I might have made two whole bucks that morning in tips. But it was cash! Cash with which I could buy gas for my car immediately. Luckily, the Karmann Ghia's minuscule engine was fuel efficient and gasoline was still 59 cents a gallon, or I might not have been able to drive home.

Over the next few weekends it slowly dawned on me that Lems was not seen as a breakfast place. It was a place to get a frosty mug of beer with your supper, but not as a place for morning waffles. I bided my long and boring shifts by digging through a toy chest near the waitress stand, from which kids could choose a cheap gewgaw if they had behaved well during their meal. From there I gleaned a small collection of hideous, rubber, finger-puppet monsters, the more poorly painted the better. I used these to decorate the dashboard of my beloved Karmann

Ghia. Though their translucent orange tentacles waved cheerily as we bounced along the streets, I could see that I wasn't getting any closer to making my first auto loan payment to my Dad. In fact, aside from the money I had spent on gas, I had next to nothing. I had no choice but to give the manager two week's notice of intent to quit. Not surprisingly, he gave me no argument.

On my last Sunday at Lems, it was pouring rain. An hour went by, and no-one came into the restaurant at all. The sky was very dark and the cold rain came down in torrents. After a while, the cook came out front and asked if I wanted some breakfast. I told him I couldn't afford it, but he shook his head and said he'd make us both some anyway, for free. He cooked us up a big spread of breakfast items and we took them to the best table in the place, in the front window, and sat down to eat. He told me all about his home in South America and we smoked cigarettes and watched the rain, the traffic, and the whole world pass slowly by Lems in the gloom. He was a perfect gentleman. I didn't make a penny in tips that last day, but I went home with a warm feeling about how nice people can be, even lonely immigrants far from home.

Since those days I have always been careful to tip the wait staff, knowing how much the money means to them. I never did quite pay off the car and eventually had to give it back to my Dad, but ever since those days I have had a soft spot in my heart for cute Karmann Ghias and ugly little rubber monsters.

Chapter Three
STOCK CLERK

The mid 1970's was an interesting time to be a teenager. Hippies were still around, and punk rockers were just emerging. I went to an alternative high school (called a charter school, now) where blue jeans and long hair walked side by side with jack boots and safety pins. I went to that school because the regular high school was lost on me. I may not have graduated, had I not gone to the alternative school. I got my history credit by using dead fish as fertilizer, in the colonial garden we planted in the school's side yard. It was a great school and I had good friends there. One of them was Kip.

Kip was a nice guy. I had known him since our days in the local children's theater. He was funny, unassuming, and introspective. One day he told me that the health food place, where he was working, was looking for another part time stock clerk and that he'd put in a good word for me if I was interested. It was the last half of my senior year of high school. The great mystery of adulthood loomed before me. My car needed gas. I was interested! So he helped me land the job.

In the 1970's there were two kinds of health-food stores. One kind of health food store was often grungy and smelly, usually run by hippies, and sold all kinds of wilted vegetables and mysterious, beige beverages. I loved that kind of health food store. The other kind was basically a chain store vitamin emporium with a sideline of non-perishable foodstuffs. This was the sort of store at which I became a stock clerk.

Our store was in a shopping center called Parkingland, which was like a multi-storied garage with semi-covered sidewalks to the shops. All of us who worked at the health food store were required to wear lab coats to make us look like health professionals, even if we were just pimply-faced high schoolers. There were two other pimply-faced high school stock clerks besides myself; my friend Kip and a guy named Tom. We had a lot of fun creeping up and down the aisles with our lab coats and clipboards making smart-aleck remarks to each other.

Being a stock clerk is a pretty laid-back job. We didn't have to deal with customers, but being friendly, we did talk to them and help them find things in the store. Mostly we took stock of what was on the shelves, checking the items off on our clipboards, noting the quantities and checking the expiration dates. When new shipments came in, we would price the items and place them on the shelves. Some times we would make displays, or hand-made signs. This is how I found out that Tom was an artist.

Tom had made a sign for banana chips (apparently more healthful than potato chips for some reason), and had included on it a small drawing of an ape face and a tiny word balloon with the caption "Yum!" This was charming, but it was only the tip of the iceberg. I was asked to take some garbage to the trash room, a job that I was not eager to do, being a klutzy teenaged girl in a white lab coat. However, the task was required of me, so off I went. The trash room was a mysterious place, a long hall between two of the stores closed off by a door that required a key. All the trash from the surrounding stores was placed there to wait for the garbage pickup. It smelled pretty funky, but as my eyes adjusted to the low light, I found upon the drywall a series of amazing life-sized portraits of the characters from "Planet of the Apes" drawn with magic marker. I recognized the style, and I knew that Tom had drawn them. It was like a "Planet of the Apes" mural in there. I don't know how he found the time to do them. I guessed that he had managed to work on them bit by bit. Either that or he had spent a lot of time in the trash room. (Maybe that was why I was sent there instead of him!) The apes were wonderfully rendered, and I always looked forward to going to the trash room after that. I made a drawing there, too. It was a character of mine named Maggolita, a cartoon maggot with Farrah Fawcett hair and cleavage, wearing an evening gown and pearls. Decades later, Parkingland was torn down and rebuilt as a modern mall, so I guess Maggolita and the Apes are long gone.

Our manager was a pretty Chinese lady by the name of May. She looked like she was in her twenties but she was really in her forties. She was a very sweet person and calmly put up with a lot of nonsense from the clerks. She had a charming Chinese accent that we all loved. We had a promotion for a Vitamin C tablet that May had to memorize word for word from a script. It was designed to entice people to try a sample and then buy two bottles for the price of one, plus one cent. We stock clerks never tired of hearing her recite

the spiel with her adorable accent. Whenever she would begin it, we would excitedly beckon to each other, then tiptoe over to hide in a parallel aisle to eavesdrop. She had this wonderful way of saying the final word: "penny", all drawn out as if it might be a sort of magical incantation. "Want to try chewable vitamin C?" she would start, "Tastes really good. On one penny sale. Buy first bottle for regular price, get second bottle for …
penny." Kip, Tom and I would silently mouth the words along with her, and when she got to "…*penny*" we would stop and freeze in place, so as not to disturb the ecstasy of the moment. Then we would scuttle back to our clipboards, satisfied.

The front part of our store was mostly vitamins, but the back had bulk teas and flours, and a vast array of snacks that were rumored to be much healthier to eat than, say, the average snack at a convenience store. To help convince our customers to try these snacks, there were many containers of samples sitting out. These contained things like seaweed sticks that tasted like salted wood, and carob drops that tasted like dirt mixed with honey. This may not sound too enticing to you, but we were high schoolers coming right to our job from classes, and we were hungry. We gobbled these treats down, then promptly reported that the samples were getting low and needed refilling. May would sometimes scold us gently for emptying the sample cups, but she understood. Sometimes, with a sly smile and a wink, she would cop a snack, herself.

A snack item that seemed to be in eternal promotion there, was an small bag of shelled sunflower seeds that went by the name of

'TASTIES'. These sunflower seeds were always in the sample cups and they were pretty good. We should know, we ate plenty of them. But they were just sunflower seeds with salt and spices, nothing too phenomenal. So we three stock clerks made up a little song about them, which we figured out how to sing in three part harmony, and it went like this:

"TASTIES are the very best,

They got more protein than the rest,

So buy yourself a bag today

and be healthy the TASTY way!

Mmmmmmmmmmmm.... TASTIES!"

We fantasized about popping our heads over the counter and singing it to unsuspecting customers, but decided it might be better not to startle anyone. We did, however, sing it to a salesman who worked there for a while. He made up a counter-melody using the ingredients as lyrics. It went something like this:

"Sunflower seeds, salt, MSG.

Corn syrup solids, Citric Acid,

Malic and Lactic Acid, Sodium Diacetate

Iodine? IODINE!

Mmmmmmmmmmmm... TASTIES!"

...which was brilliant, but of course he never sang that for customers either, because he didn't want them to know the ingredients, he just wanted them to buy the darned things.

The school year ended and I had to quit to go to college, but I look back at my health food stock clerk days fondly. I lost track of May and the salesman, but am still in contact with Kip. With his love of "Planet of the Apes", Tom toyed with movie-making. I helped him with one, a vampire movie that we filmed in an abandoned funeral home. I played a corpse. I pestered Tom for a while to see the finished film, but somehow he was always too busy to show it to me. Rumor had it that as I was lying on a steel table covered with catsup, Tom scootched my shroud and tube top down way more than I would have allowed, had I known, and he was afraid I'd be mad. The thanks I got for this generous contribution to cinematography was to walk six miles home covered in catsup. I stuck my thumb out, but no-one seemed anxious to give me a lift, for some reason. Tom went on to become a special effects make-up artist and "cheesecake" photographer. I recently found out that he had died at the age of 56. So much for all that health food.

Chapter Four
WAITRESS

The ad in the paper announced part-time employment opportunities for enthusiastic, experienced servers for a new French Cafe in an underground mall. The pay started at $100 per week plus tips. After my $1 an hour part-time waitress stint, this sounded like a fantastic deal. I called for an interview, polished myself up and went and got hired.

The restaurant owner, a jovial Greek fellow, called a meeting of the new wait staff. The four of us waited quite some time for him to show up, began to get acquainted, and luckily all got along quite well. Carla, a tall, pretty young woman who looked like a model but was in college and had a student loan to pay off, said she didn't care what happened in this job as long as she got her hundred bucks a week. Angie, a short, young, attractive brunette with large flirty eyes, had a young child to raise on her own. She had worked at a popular French restaurant in Georgetown and really knew a thing or two about French cuisine. Ross was a terribly good looking young man who proudly announced his recent crowning as Washington D.C.'s 'Little Mister Gay Universe'. He was just there to make money to buy clothes. By the time the boss came in, we were all talking like we'd known each other for years.

Our boss described his vision for the restaurant. It had been a cafeteria, but he had received permission to extend the dining room outside the storefront and into the mall area near a fountain, which was pretty nice. We were all to wear white button-down shirts and black slacks, bow ties, black leather shoes and crisp white aprons. After a few jobs with ugly polyester uniforms, it was rather fun to be able to take pride in my appearance. Each day we would have secret contests for who had the coolest bowtie.

There were three other employees at the French Cafe. One was a cook, whom we rarely saw, as he was trapped back in the pristine, white kitchen, behind a counter with a rotating drum on which we clipped the orders. Next, there was a strange little hunchbacked busboy who was probably in his forties, barely spoke a word of English and was clearly not all there, upstairs. Lastly, there was the cashier, a heavy blonde woman with thick glasses who rarely smiled and appeared to be of the opinion that she looked like Bo

Derek in the movie "10". She wore a plastic barrette in her hair every single day, from which dangled a set of artificial cornrow style braids that did not quite match her hair. The waiters were glad she was there, though, because it meant that we didn't have to total up any checks. We just brought them to her, she entered them in the register, we returned with the customer's payment and she gave us the change. Piece of cake.

Tips were okay, but were always shared with the cook, cashier and busboy. I was a very conscientious waitperson and tried hard to please the customers. Still, the one who got the highest tips was always Ross, who rolled his handsome eyes at people, apparently giving them that authentic 'rude French waiter' experience. They loved him.

This particular waitstaff was so tight knit that we sometimes hung out together after shifts. We would haunt the underground mall together, sometimes stopping at a bar for a drink with some of our tip money. Ross had a crush on one of the guys in the Gentleman's Jodhpur clothing store, and liked to parade us past it, laughing gaily and pretending to be highly distracted by all his female companions. This was his idea of flirting. We thought this was loads of fun.

We got very little, if any, supervision. Our boss would appear only occasionally from his office down the hall, and would look generally happy with us. His wife was a tiny but formidable woman, always coifed to the nines and dressed to the tens in ornate Hermes scarves and lots of gold jewelry. When the mood struck her, she would clack into the kitchen on her high heels to shriek at the bus-boy and the cook, but never at the waiters, thank goodness. My sister, who speaks fluent Greek, visited the cafe once, could hear her all the way out in the dining area, and could understand the names she was calling them. Since none of the other customers' hair was standing on end, we gratefully assumed that they did not understand Greek.

Time went by and perhaps the charm wore off, but we began to get complaints from the customers. "This eggs Benedict is STONE COLD!" one woman barked at me. I, of course, apologized profusely, but inwardly I was rolling my eyes like Ross. How could they be 'stone cold' when I had just picked them up from the kitchen? I trotted the dish back to the cook who just shrugged and stuck it in the microwave for another minute or so.

It was then that I realized that the food had literally been frozen solid only minutes ago. No wonder the kitchen area was always so clean! It wasn't being used for cooking!

The other waiters and I were a bit embarrassed to have figured this out, but what could we do? We wanted our paychecks, and would just have to hold up our heads and hope that no-one asked us if the food was prepared fresh.

One fine day I popped in on my day off to pick up my paycheck on the way to the bank. The boss saw me and waved me into his office. He told me frankly that he could no longer afford to keep a wait staff, and that 'Bo Derek' had been embezzling from the cash register. He appreciated how polite and honest I was, so he was going to keep me on

44

as cashier and fire 'Bo', Carla, Ross and Angie right after their shift was over that day. Uneasily, I thanked him and walked out with my check.

I didn't know what to think. I was perhaps a little flattered that I was to survive as an employee there, but then I thought about Ross' need for clothes, Carla's student loan, and Angie's little kid, and my blood ran as cold as frozen eggs Benedict. There they were in the dining room, slaving away, with no idea that they would soon be out of work. I stopped in my tracks. Then I turned around.

I found each waiter and we made a huddle in the middle of the floor. I told them that they were all going to be fired and that I was to become cashier, only that I didn't plan on showing up because I thought it was a crummy way to treat people. They were very grateful to hear about this before it happened, and we all stood there hugging in a circle, knowing we would probably never see each other again. The strange little hunchbacked busboy spied us from the kitchen and, beaming with childlike joy, ran eagerly out to us with his arms outstretched. He wanted to be in on the hug, too. We let him in on the hug, laughed a sad laugh about it, and broke off to deal with the rest of the day.

I don't know if they stayed the rest of their shift, or dragged their aprons on the floor on the way out, which according to Angie is the way proud waiters show their distain in such situations. All I know is I never went back there to work, or to eat, again.

Chapter Five

ANSWERING PHONES

When one is a freelance artist, one sometimes has dry spells between paying art jobs,
when the phone doesn't ring for an extended
period of time. It was during one of these
times, as my checkbook balance dwindled
and my rent payment loomed on the horizon,
that I found myself a job answering phones.

The company that hired me specialized in
sending a happy mime with a bunch of balloons to a client's doorstep. It was enjoying
some wild popularity at the time, having recently been written up by a major newspaper.
So it came to be that I found myself in a win-
dowless room with three other people, pick-

ing up phones and taking orders for these deliveries.

The work was not challenging, but I enjoyed the company of my three co-workers. One was a guy named Gus, who had deep circles under his eyes and always wore an expression that said "just shoot me now". Everything he uttered was the most depressing thing possible for the moment. He was so depressing it was almost genius. For some reason I found this humorous, and would laugh at these droll comments. This would cause him to stare at me with his hang-dog, dead-eyed face and make me laugh all the more. Another colleague was Bertha, a very large woman with a sweet temper and a charming southern drawl. She was a good contrast to Gus. The two of them were like the proverbial angel and devil that sit on your shoulders. The third phone operator was a guy named Frank. Frank was a pleasant, cheerful fellow, and a really wonderful artist.

Our cell was around 12 by 15 feet, and had folding chairs and a long counter with phones, pens and order pads. On the wall was a sign saying: "SMILE! They can hear you." (Gus never smiled, but he somehow stayed employed there. Maybe he was related to the owners.) There were also lots of sticky-notes all over the walls with various information about credit card companies and the like. Hidden among these were some absolutely fabulous ball-point pen drawings by Frank. These were just little doodles he would come up with as he waited for phone calls. His favorite subject was hideous monsters devouring people, with lots of guts and blood. Whenever Frank finished one, he would always show it to Bertha and she would always exclaim, "Oh Frank, that's just *horrible!*", which delighted him almost to tears. He confided in me that he drew them just to hear her say that.

Frank and I would try to impress each other by making little flip-book cartoons in the corners of our order pads. To make a flip book, you draw a little drawing on each page, each drawing slightly different from the previous, so when you flip the pages in rapid succession, it looks as if the drawings move. We would make cartoons of anvils dropping on clown's heads and babies being swallowed by aliens, that sort of thing, and we'd always show Bertha, and she'd always say they were just *horrible*.

One busy weekend when it was just the guys and me there, one of the delivery mimes came down with the flu and had to go home. This was an emergency because we had a big order going out to a child's party that afternoon. The only other mime on duty that day was on a call way out in the far suburbs, and couldn't possibly make it back in time. Neither Frank nor I had authorization to operate a company van, so we had to send Gus. I'll never forget Gus standing at the door getting ready to leave with his khaki slacks rolled up over his hairy knees, and rainbow suspenders over his button-down shirt. In his hand were two dozen brightly colored balloons, but his pallid, sad-sack face wore the expression of a man going to meet his doom. He was decidedly un-festive. Frank and I took one look at him and burst into laughter. Gus' sunken eyes glowered under the whimsical flowered hat. "Screw you people," he pouted, and off he went, humiliated, with his bunch of bright balloons cascading behind him. After he returned, I asked him what the clients had said when they saw him. "They didn't say anything, they just took their balloons and closed the door, " he muttered. Again, Frank and I laughed as Gus sank, expressionless, into his folding chair.

We got all kinds of phone calls from all kinds of people, most of them very happy, because sending balloons is a happy thing. Some of the balloons we offered has messages on them, like "Happy Birthday", "Get Well," and "I Love You". When I read the list of options to one lady, she very much objected to the one which said "You Were Great Last Night!". She thought it was indecent, and hung up on me. I guess she couldn't imagine sending it to an actor who had just survived opening night, but oh well. Sometimes you just can't tell when people will choose to be offended. There was also the guy on the phone who was ordering "I Love You" balloons for his girlfriend, and suddenly started to flirt with me. "You have a beautiful voice. You must be a beautiful lady," he purred into the phone, "What time do you get off work?" After politely refusing several advances, I somehow convinced him that I was an eighty-five-year-old hag, and managed to complete the sale. I hoped that his lady friend knew what she was getting into with him.

It was nice to have a regular paycheck. One day on my way back home from work I found myself at a funky little hipster boutique that sold clothes and accessories to the rock club crowd. It was the early 1980's and the punk era was in full swing. I decided to have some fun and treated myself to some turquoise green hair dye. My hair was all ready short and bleached white, so it absorbed that green dye in no time. It was a brilliant color, like the fur of a new plush toy. I was very pleased with the results and had a fun Saturday night showing it off. I got a lot of compliments at the punk rock club.

My co-workers were amazed at my new hair color, but when our boss (who we rarely saw) passed by our cell, he stopped and wordlessly beckoned to me to follow him into his office. Once there, he told me that my green hair had to go. "But our customer never see me anyway!" I protested. He wouldn't budge on the subject. I felt he was just wielding power to make himself feel important. "That is ridiculous. I quit," I told him, and left my job, scoring one for the underdog and feeling totally punk rock.

I was disappointed when my beautiful green hair color washed out in about a week, but I didn't go back to the phone cell. I had made my point, there. Soon enough, a freelance illustration job did come my way. One where only the work mattered, not the color of my hair.

Chapter Six

MEDICAL FILMS

I learned the art of hand-drawn cel animation through an apprenticeship with a well-known Washington D.C. animator in the early 1980's. Making cartoons on film is not a colossal industry in the district, and most of the projects we worked on were short commercial bits and rather dry presentations for various government agencies. After a couple of years of learning the craft, my mentor decided that I needed the experience of working in a big commercial studio, and he got me a job with a large company that made medical films on the far outskirts of Baltimore. At first I commuted there, going from bus to subway to commuter train to bus again in each direction. It was time-consuming, expensive and exhausting. Miraculously, my mentor's wife found it in her heart to sell me her old car, a 1972 four door Thunderbird .that had been recently crashed into by a guy having a heart attack while it was parked on their street. It had a very unsightly crunched back fender, but was otherwise drivable, and a steal at only $50. It also had a powerful engine, rear suicide doors (that opened backwards), and turn signals that winked in a sequence of lights. I dubbed it The Mothership.

The Mothership's maiden voyage was to my job at the medical film company by way of the Washington beltway, and then on to the Baltimore beltway. This was long before electronic navigation in cars, so I had the directions written on a piece of paper taped to the dashboard. Getting there took about two hours in crazy beltway traffic, but I made it there alive, just barely. Getting home was another two hours in crazy beltway traffic. I was leaving at seven in the morning and getting home at seven at night, but I was young and able to tolerate it, in order to pay my dues as a film studio hack.

You are probably wondering what a cartoon animator was doing at a medical film studio. I wondered that, too. The place was massive, a huge warehouse in which one could get lost rather easily. I didn't explore it much, just made my way to the animation department each day and got to work. The head animators were two great older fellahs, Art and Bertram. Art was a warm, grounded, quiet man who loved to listen to 1940's jazz and swing music at his desk. He was a good friend of my mentor, and took me under his wing. Bertram was more eccentric. He had a shock of white hair and like to bob around the department humming under his breath. My cubicle was near a snack machine, and every day Bertram would come by several times to talk to the snacks. One day I heard him sigh "Everything good is gone." He then made up a little song on that theme: "Everything good is gone- wackadoo, wackadoo, wackadoo... oh shit." That song has remained with me ever since.

There were three other people in the animation department. Two of them were younger than me and didn't seem to have much to talk about except what was on TV and what they were going to have for dinner that night. They discussed this at regular intervals, several times daily, beginning at approximately 9:12 a.m. They were nice enough people, just not tremendously interesting to me. The third person was a small middle aged lady who had a foreign accent and didn't say much at first. I just assumed she was shy. One day I stopped by her desk and spent quite some time there listening to the remarkable story of how she defected from a central European country with nothing but the coat on her back, the sleeve linings of which contained some family jewelry to help her get started in America. She had been through a lot, but had a sweet personality. I liked her.

My first assignment was to work on a film about intestinal laparoscopy. Through the miracle of animation I was to illustrate a tiny camera on a tube moving through a bowel. I truly enjoyed creating the background illustrations of the twisty-turny intestines, and spent a blissful week or so delicately shading and highlighting my masterpiece using high quality colored pencils. People would stop by my desk to ooh and ahh at my intestines. The actual animated drawings of the laparoscope winding through them were comparatively boring (so to speak). So that's what a medical animator does: creates drawn footage of guts and other anatomical parts and diseases for instructional films. It was pretty interesting work. Plus, no-one ever seemed to check up on me or what I was doing. I just got the work and did it and if I had a question I would ask Art or Bertram about it. In between assignments, I just did whatever I wanted. At one point I created a comic called "Bertram's Believe It or Not", showing good old Bertram being wowed by various mundane things around the office. I hung this cartoon in the animation camera room, and was later gratified to hear people laughing at it from down the hall.

Being a bit of an introvert, most days I just ate lunch at my desk, but on Fridays all the employees were treated to a free meal in the lunchroom. It was usually tuna or egg salad sandwiches, but it was free and it got us out of our little departments so that we could socialize. It was a lovely thing to do, but there was one custodian who felt it was in my best interest to know what he thought of my appearance. He felt that I should wear dresses, get my hair done and wear make-up. I guess he didn't think I was attractive enough for his tastes. Too bad. I told him that I had mistakenly left my tiara and white gloves in my other purse. He did not get my joke. Since I spent all day drawing guts I did not feel the need to dress like Trisha Nixon at a tea party, but I was never able to convince him of this.

Eventually I was offered some freelance work back in the Washington D.C. area and decided that I had had enough of studio grunt work, so I handed in my resignation. The place was so huge and impersonal they didn't even blink at my leaving. I was just a drop in the bucket to them. I said goodbye, shook hands and was wished well.

It was raining very heavily as I left that evening and the Mothership, having a complex electrical system, chose to stall in a deep puddle right in the middle of the first busy intersection I entered. Being unable to see more than twenty feet ahead of me in the downpour, and rattled by all the impatient drivers honking at me, I managed to take a wrong turn and eventually wound up in downtown Baltimore. As the rain eased up, I found I was hopelessly lost. To top it off, it happened to be Saint Patrick's Day evening. At one point I found myself on Charles Street being vigorously honked at again. A bunch of large, old drunk guys in sparkly green bowler hats were dancing in front of my car and I had stopped to avoid hitting them. They danced, horns blared and I put my head on the Mothership's steering wheel and nearly wept. Not only was I lost and being harassed by other drivers, I was also in danger of running over giant drunken leprechauns, in the rain, on Saint Patrick's Day. Perhaps it was through the luck of the Irish that I found my way through Baltimore, and out to the complete opposite side of the beltway from which I had started. Never before had I been so relieved to see the Washington Capitol dome appear on the horizon. It was 9pm before I ate my dinner that night, but I was grateful to be home and didn't even think about going out for green beer. I felt lucky enough just to have made it back safely. The large film studio experience was behind me now, fading away like a sweet old song: "wackadoo, wackadoo, wackadoo…"

Chapter Seven

DRAWING FOR THE GOVERNMENT

I had created a series of animated public
service announcements for the U.S. Department of the Interior. These were short cartoon
television commercials in which various an-
imals advised people to keep their national
parks free of litter. While that may not sound
too fascinating, it was pretty thrilling for me
because it was the first freelance animation
job I had done entirely on my own. The characters were all my own designs and I had
personally drawn each frame of motion and
filmed it myself. The clients were pleased
with my work and it kept me paid for the better part of a year, which for a freelance artist
is a very good gig.

The blush from that small success was still on the rose, so to speak, when I received a call from someone at the Department of the Interior asking if I could do a small illustration job for them. I told them that I would be delighted. So it was with some sense of accomplishment that I entered the doors of the huge old Interior Building in Washington D.C. the next day, after some confusion over which door I was supposed to enter through, of course. The Interior Building is massive. If you were to get a bird's eye view of it, it might look like a few gigantic capital letter H's linked together through the middle dash. There are several floors, and each floor has several long wings of offices. I took an elevator to the correct floor, but once there I had no clue as to where to find the office at which I was expected. People in suits were walking briskly around, much too busy to make eye contact with an out-of-place artist in an un-comfortable dress that she imagined looked professional when she put it on, but now was not so sure about that. I was standing dumbly in the middle of the hall trying to figure out the direction sign, when I heard a beeping noise. I stepped out of the way just in time to avoid being bumped into by a long, un-manned file cabinet on wheels that was slow-ly making its way down the corridor. There was a flashing light perched on top of it, along with a card which read "BLINKY". As it passed, people would pop out of offices to retrieve files from it, or put files onto it. I guess that BLINKY was some sort of early earth-bound version of a drone. It looked so strange and cumbersome I just had to laugh at it. "What the HECK is going on around here?" I must have said out loud, because a passing person heard me, told me about

BLINKY (there were apparently several of them in the building) and kindly offered me directions to my destination.

The man I had been sent to see was some sort of director of employee relations or something. He was gruff, middle aged, heavy, smelled like cigarettes and, in short, was everything I'd dreamed he would be, judging from his voice on the phone. He really liked to hear himself talk, and peppered our meeting with comments about different people as they passed by in the hall. "That guy is a dumbass," he'd suddenly say, or "She's built like a brick shit-house." I kind of wished that he would get to the point so I could just go home, get the work done and get paid, but that was not to be.

Eventually, he got around to explaining that he needed a drawing of a buffalo standing on its hind legs and leaning an elbow on the official seal of the Department of the Interior (which I didn't have to draw, thank goodness- they would paste in a photo of it.) This was supposed to illustrate a pamphlet about employee benefits. He explained that the buffalo had to look friendly and cartoony, but not too cartoony. He had to look like a real buffalo, like the one on the seal of the Interior, but not too real. In short, he shouldn't have a "wee-wee". Okay, so I needed to draw a cartoony but realistic, friendly buffalo standing on his hind legs without a "wee-wee". Got it. All I had to do was to run along home and create it. But this wasn't going to happen. Not yet.

He then began to tell me about other projects he had in mind, some cartoon ideas he had. These ideas seemed to me to be to be rather stale, but he was unaware of this. He continued by bragging about the many projects he had previously accomplished. Suddenly he jumped up. "Oh good, he's done," I thought, but instead, he wanted to show me a recording studio elsewhere in the building. At least I was up off the chair, maybe I could bow out quickly as soon as I saw the studio. It turns out he had edited an Independence Day music program featuring recordings of the Army Navy Band, and was very proud of the results. Did I want to hear it? No, I wanted to go home and get to work, but he played it anyway. As I sat there listening to bombastic patriotic music while he conducted with an imaginary baton, I felt my mind leave my body to retrace my steps back out of the Interior building, in case I got half a chance to make a dash for the exit. My neck was stiff from enthusiastic nodding and my jaw hurt from the fake smile I had plastered on my face to keep from yawning, so it was with a rather uncomfortable jolt that I was yanked back to my body when the music abruptly ended. "It's time to call it a day," he said, "Where are you headed? I'll give you a lift home." My mind raced to figure out a good excuse as to why I would prefer to use the subway, but having only being recently reconnected with the rest of me, it balked. "Great, thanks," I said.

On the way home, the guy suggested that we stop for drinks, but I told him that I had to go meet my boyfriend of five years. He pouted and stewed about that for a few minutes, which was great because it prevented him from talking. He had apparently wanted something more from me than mere gratitude. I was vaguely disappointed with myself for being so naive as to think that an offer of a ride home meant simply that. He too, obviously, held me responsible for his lack of clarity. He left me off at the end of my driveway. "You're not getting any younger, you know," he told me by way of a farewell.

I drew the buffalo the next day and opted to send it in rather than appear again in person. The guy called me a few days later and said that it looked great, but the department had had a meeting about it and decided that it probably should have had a "wee-wee" after all. I somehow convinced him to move the Department of the Interior seal over a little, to conceal the "wee-wee" area so it would not be an issue. I was relieved when he agreed to do so. A check came in the mail a month later.

I never did another project with that guy, but when all was said and done I suppose I did get something out of the whole experience. I realized that, in fact, I was not getting any younger, and with a renewed appreciation for the difference between a jerk and a gentleman, I finally made my boyfriend my husband a few months later.

Chapter Eight
FLORAL DESIGN

I had passed the sign in the shop window for nearly a month. "WANTED: FLORAL DESIGNER" it read. My husband and I had bought a small house in a small town almost a year previous to this, and I had planted a garden and had played with arranging flowers with some success, but I had no professional experience. Still, I needed a job and the artistic nature of this field appealed to me. So I got some books and I read about the principals of floral design, and I bought equipment and experimented on my own for about a week. When I headed back to the flower shop, I was sure that the position had been taken, but the sign was still there, so in I went.

I explained my situation to June, the owner, and she decided to give me an audition. "Make a centerpiece with these items," she said, putting a bowl, wet floral foam, and a bunch of ferns and flowers on the table. I went to work taping down the foam in the bowl, then added the greenery and finally, the flowers, as I had learned the previous week. When I turned to ask June if it was okay, she was gone. I found her out front, taking the help wanted sign out of the window. I had been hired.

June was a nice, petite lady and a very patient boss. She was the perfect person for me to work for, because she knew nearly everyone in town, while I was still new in the area.

I got to meet many local people at the shop. People would call her for arrangements and she would know just what to make, what style to use and what colors to choose. She knew what color everyone's dining room was painted, and would make arrangements based on that. June was also very sentimental and would weep while taking orders for funerals because she personally knew the grief stricken families. She also cried for wedding arrangements. She knew all the local gossip. It struck me as awfully generous of her, when she would mention certain not-so-savory characters, to finish her comments with "bless their hearts". How sweet of her, I thought.

June taught me techniques I hadn't seen in my instruction books; things like wiring roses, which is a way of giving support to roses with thin stems by winding wire around them. She also taught me how to cut flowers with a jackknife. The theory at the time was that snipping stems with scissors pinched the ends so that they couldn't draw water efficiently, and would wither more quickly. So we sliced stems with little Swiss army knives. I had so many scores on my fingers those first weeks that I wondered if my fingerprints were still recognizable. During down times at the shop June and I would study the floral trade magazines to see what new ideas we could find. Sometimes we would try an unusual design just to see if it sold. I really enjoyed this sort of thing.

After a couple of weeks working as a floral designer I celebrated a day off by attempting to make candles. Unfortunately I did not study up on candle-making methods, as I had with flower arranging. What was there to know- you just melted some wax and poured it in a mold, right? Wrong. I used a saucepan instead of a double boiler, and the resultant four-foot flames scorched my kitchen ceiling and burned my arm. I spent an afternoon at the hospital and went home with a big bandage, feeling like a total fool. I did not miss any work, but nerve damage to my hand made it more difficult for me to do things like tie bows. June kindly tied bows for me, and sometimes when we were sitting around she would casually tie a bunch of bows in various colors, in case I needed them later. That's the kind of boss she was. Really thoughtful. Later, when the bandage came off I had a huge ugly scab on the side of my wrist, about three inches long and two inches wide. It was horrible looking, but since it needed air to heal, I left it un-bandaged. One afternoon as I handed off a large centerpiece for a fancy event, I noticed that the ugly scab had fallen off. I looked on the table and the floor, but couldn't locate it. Then it dawned on me that maybe it had fallen into the arrangement! It was too late to check though, the delivery man had left. We never heard any complaints about it, so I guess no-one noticed.

There was a town drunk that lived near the flower shop at that time. He reminded me of Otis from the old *Andy Griffith* TV shows. Occasionally, through the front window, we would see him wandering aimlessly up and down the street. One day he came and stood in the open doorway to the shop. He just stood there, gently swaying, for a very long time. It was as if he knew he shouldn't come into the shop in such a state, but he couldn't quite figure out how to back up. June was worried that he was blocking the door and that he would scare away her customers. I offered to call the police, but June said no. "He'll figure out how to leave in a little while, bless his heart," she said. And he did.

Thanksgiving time came, and I asked June if I could make a display in the front window to suggest to people that we could make their holiday centerpieces. She agreed, and I had a fun time creating a fancy mock table all set up for a feast. Maybe it worked, because on the day before Thanksgiving we worked overtime trying to keep up with all the orders. Late in the day I took a call from a person who was ordering rather pricey arrangements for several people in the area. He told me to put it on his bill. I asked June if Mr. So-an-so could be billed, and she said yes. So the arrangements were made and sent out, and we closed up shop late, tired, but happy for all the business. It wasn't until weeks later that an irate man called and said that he had been billed for things he had not ordered. It turned out that the man was a landlord and his disgruntled tenants, whom he was evicting, had made the orders in his name. Of course we couldn't ask him to pay for what he had not ordered, so the flower shop had to absorb the loss. June, flustered at the incident, blamed me for not paying attention. I felt terrible for accepting the order, but it really wasn't my fault. June quickly apologized when she saw that I was taken aback. "Those people thought they were getting back at their landlord," she said, "but all they really did was rip off the flower shop. Bless their hearts." It was then that I realized that "bless their hearts" does not always mean "bless their hearts".

I was redeemed later, when a famous local artist had double bypass heart surgery and we got many calls from people near and far, sending get well wishes. I was familiar with this man's work and his style, and even knew two people who had posed for his sculptures. I knew he loved the French Impressionists. Now, when some people order flowers, they choose the arrangement from a book of suggestions. This kind of order is really boring for floral designers, because they then have to make the arrangement look just like the photo in the book. By far the best kind of order is one where the customer trusts the creativity of the designer and just says "I want to spend X amount of dollars". Well, some generous friend of this artist called and said "Send him something for a hundred dollars". I was thrilled. I found a big, gorgeous basket made of corn husks and filled it with rich yellow sunflowers, deep green ivy, blood red gladiolas and royal blue delphiniums. I tried to make it look like Claude Monet had just come in from his garden and laid this basket on the counter. It looked great, and away it went. About a month later we got a card from the artist, telling us how much he loved that arrangement! Can you imagine? He wasn't even thanking the person that ordered it. He just appreciated the beauty of it. We proudly hung that card on the wall.

After about six months I got an offer to do a big cartoon animation job. I could work from home, and the pay was too good to pass up. I reluctantly gave June two weeks notice. She was very understanding about it. One evening as my final day neared, June wasn't feeling too great. She had had bronchitis most of the winter and the coughing had interfered with her sleep. She was exhausted and went home to rest. Our delivery guy was also down with a cold. It was a slow afternoon and I thought I had everything under control when someone called and said they needed a dozen roses delivered by 5 o'clock. It was 4:30. I called June and she said that her husband would pick up the roses at 4:45 to deliver them, but that they had to be wired because the stems were weak. I don't know if it was because of the nerve damage in my hand but I was still struggling with the wiring when June's husband came stomping in at 4:40. "Where are the flowers?" he demanded. "I have just three more to wire," I explained. "Goodbye," he said, and flounced out the door. I was flabbergasted! As his car pulled away from the curb I ran out to the sidewalk and yelled "Thanks a heap," furthermore referring to him as some sort of opening that a donkey might pass through, I am sorry to say. People on the street stared at me in disbelief, but June's husband kept right on driving. Since I had no car, June had to come up off her sick bed and deliver the flowers herself. She had been a good person to work for and the two of us remained on friendly terms afterward. Her husband, however, never apologized, and so I never had the chance to forgive him. Bless his heart.

Chapter Nine

BOOKSTORE WORK

Some sort of commotion was going on in the back yard. There was a crashing through the underbrush, dogs barking, a cat wailing. When I ran out to see what was up, I saw a large black dog with what looked like a rag in its mouth. It was not a rag, it was my cat. I ran at the dog, yelling for it to spit her out. Thank goodness, the dog obeyed and ran away. My cat was in terrible shape. Wide-eyed and pitiful, she yowled wildly at me as I approached her. She was traumatized. My husband grabbed her, wrapped her in a towel and ran her to the veterinarian's office down the street. The poor thing had been torn open on one side and needed to be stapled back together. The vet bill was pretty hefty and we needed to see if the dog's owners knew what had happened, and would help out.

I wasn't sure exactly which dog had done the damage, but I knew that a nearby bookstore often had a couple of dogs barking in the back yard, so I approached them first. I was rather worried that they might be defensive and belligerent, so I chose my words carefully. A refined, older lady greeted me, and we traded niceties for a moment or two before I asked her if she had a dog there, and if it had gotten out on the day of the incident. Her face gently fell. Yes, she admitted that the dog had gotten out and that she had heard the commotion. She apologized for the dog, and offered to pay the entire vet bill, much to my relief. Thank goodness for polite people.

A few days later she came by my house with some cans of cat food. I showed her the garden that I had started. Then she asked me if I might be interested in working at her bookstore on weekends. At that point I realized that she was just as relieved as I had been, that we had settled the problem with no further bloodshed. So that was my job interview. I went to work at the bookstore the following week.

The bookstore was in a gorgeous old house all filled with antique furniture. In the back was a lovely patio and a grand perennial garden. It was a beautiful place to work. The owners were a retired couple, a Southern Colonel who liked to tinker with old time-pieces upstairs, and his wife Alice, who ran the bookstore downstairs. They were very nice, refined people with excellent taste.

They were well-read (of course) and witty.
Their politics were completely on the other
end of the spectrum from mine, but we tend-
ed to respectfully steer away from conflicting
subjects and had still had lots of common in-
terests to talk about. There was plenty of
good literature, art and gardening to keep us
conversing in a congenial way.

The work was pleasant. I was unsupervised
and allowed to sit and read when not busy. I
helped people find books, ran the cash register, and did book searches on microfiche, a
spool of film that would come to us monthly
by mail. Each spool contained a huge amount
of microscopic book information that we
could project onto a screen to read when we
needed to look up rare books. This was before the wide use of computers. Now you can
look up any book in a flash at home, but back

then you needed microfiche. I also took phone calls and arranged for book orders by phone. There was a local estate with a huge garden library that probably kept the bookstore in business more than anyone else. There was always a tall stack of special order books on hold for them.

There were three kinds of books that sold the most in this bookstore. The first kind was the garden books. They had the most wonderful collection of classic garden authors there, and I looked forward to slow summer weekends when hardly anyone came in so I could pore through Gertrude Jekyll, Christopher Lloyd, and Henry Mitchell. I would swoon over great coffee table books filled with fabulous color photographs from the most famous gardens of the world.

Another big seller at this bookstore was the history books. Since we lived in an old historic southern town we had a lot of local interest in the Civil War. There was a Confederate flag (among others) hanging on the front of the building, which made me a bit uneasy, but I reasoned away that it was because of all our Civil War books. We had lots of Civil War buffs coming in looking for material on the subject. One man was looking for a particular volume, and I showed him to our Civil War shelf. "There was nothing civil about it!" he admonished me irritably, "It was The War of Aggression from the North!" I did not attempt to argue with him.

The third most popular place in the bookstore was the children's book room, which was upstairs, in what had once been a sleeping porch. The wooden floors were painted sage green and slanted slightly down toward a pretty view of the garden below. The low shelves had wonderful books for children. I remember sitting on the floor and reading *Crow Boy* by Taro Yashima. It is a sweet book about a little poor boy who gets teased at school until the class hears how well he can imitate birds. It made me cry. Luckily, no-one was in the store at the time of this outburst. I wound up buying the book for a dear friend.

I did not make a lot of money working at the bookstore, but I could walk there, so I had no transportation expenses. There were three other women that worked there part time and I think we each made $5 per hour. We did get a 25% discount on books, which was great, except that it was so tempting to spend the entire paycheck on discounted books. I happily filled in for the other employees whenever they were out sick, or wanted a vacation. The store rarely became hectic. Every once in a while we would have a book signing which would bring in a crowd, and the weeks before Christmas were busy as well, but usually it was easy to keep up with tasks. Since my regular hours were only on weekends, I could accept small freelance art jobs during the week. It was a pretty good deal for me.

The garden out back was like a small paradise. Pale pink roses climbed the trellises and spilled out over the pergola that shaded the patio. Irises and peonies swayed in the spring breezes and oriental lilies glowed in the summer sunshine. One time some out-of-towners stopped in and asked where they could have a picnic. I sent them out to the garden and they had such a lovely time out there that they came back in afterward and bought some books. There was a massive rosemary shrub growing against the back of the house and after the occasional rude customer I would flee to it, sweep my hand across it and be instantly soothed by its heavenly aroma. I would help Alice make flower arrangements from the garden for special events. We dressed the little staircase up in magnolia leaves once and it looked fabulous.

Early on, I noticed that the book store never seemed to do anything with their front window, so I asked if I could dress it up for them. They were doing a promotion where customers would get a free cloth book bag with a certain purchase amount. They had boxes of these nice-looking book bags with a nice quote about reading printed on them, and not enough of them were going out the door. I made up the window with the bags filled with books, falling over and spilling books, I even hung book bags from the ceiling like party decorations. The window got a lot of compliments, and many book bags found good homes that holiday season.

Once Alice found out that I could draw, she would often ask me to make a cute sign for a sale, which was fun for me. She did step a bit over the line when she asked me to come in on my day off to draw daffodils for a tea party she was hosting. I thought I would draw the flowers once, and then go home. It turned out she meant that I was to hand-draw daffodils on each of at least fifty invitations. It took over four hours (on my day off!), and she still paid me only my shop girl wage of $5 an hour for it. That was quite a bit below my regular rate for illustration. I made a mental note to make sure I understood the terms before I would agree to do anything like that again.

Other than that, the only thing that bugged me much about working there was the presence of an old children's book that had timed out of its copyright, so the store owners had bought the rights to it. This was a book about a small black child who had a run-in with a tiger, and in itself the story was neither that good nor bad. The problem was mostly that the illustrations were rather grotesque caricatures of a boy with ink black skin and big red lips, and I knew full well that the title character's name had been used as a racial epithet for many years. The dialogue of the book was unfortunately written in a colloquial form that was unmistakably poking fun at how black people used to talk in the southern

United States. The owners insisted that it was a classic children's story and not at all offensive, that it was instead a heroic tale that took place in India, because that is where tigers live. I wasn't convinced, but I liked my job and figured that it was not my business to agree with the presence of every book in the store. When people were looking for books on my watch, I always steered them clear of this particular one. I did mention to Alice about the time when two worldly young black women stumbled across it, were absolutely appalled, plunked down the books they were going to buy and left the store. I thought I'd die of embarrassment. Alice just had a "you can't please everyone" attitude about it. We argued politely back and forth about the book every once in a while, but they were not about to admit that their investment was anything short of proper.

The problem arose, however, when the owners decided to publish a large anniversary edition of the book. I stayed out of it, but when it came out, Alice asked me to make a big poster for the front of the store, featuring the main character. Feeling my hackles rise, I did not answer her right away for fear the conversation should become too shrill. I sat at the desk wondering how the heck I was going to talk my way out of the task at hand. Then I recalled Alice teasing me once that people on my end of the political spectrum (I'm not saying which side, but I'm sure you've all ready guessed) have no backbone. So I straightened my backbone and went to talk with her. I explained that I would not be making the poster for her. She asked why. I told her that it was because I felt that the subject was demeaning to black people and that I

could not, in good conscience, use my talents
to promote it. She said that there was nothing
wrong with the book. I admitted that I would
be uncomfortable making the poster. There
was a pause. "Then maybe you would be
more comfortable working elsewhere," she
said softly. "Maybe I would," I quietly answered, almost surprised to hear the words
coming out of my mouth. Then I went back
to my desk and wrote a letter of resignation.
My last two weeks there were uneventful.
Alice and I never mentioned the incident
again. I knew that we were both sorry about
the end of my employment there, but I also
knew that we were both too stubborn to back
down about it. In some ways we were very
much alike.

Weeks passed, and one day I saw an article
in a local newspaper about the bookstore

owners and the grand re-release of the book. Alice was quoted as saying that no-one she knew of had ever objected to the book! I was mildly shocked, but not too surprised by this. I thought to write to the newspaper editor, but decided that it was enough to just let her denial stew in her conscience. I know she had one.

A couple of years later the bookstore went out of business, receding in time like a quaint memory, and most of the memories I have of working there are good ones. Most of them.

Chapter Ten
SCOOPING ICE CREAM

A notice in our local paper called for volunteers to help organize our town's bicentennial celebration and, eager to be of some use, I attended the planning meeting. That is how a woman named Lani and I somehow talked ourselves into taking charge of the craft fair.

Lani was good natured, and large in stature. To some, she may have seemed heavy-set, however her waist did swoop inward between her broad shoulders and hips. Her dark hair was cropped short but she told me she used to wear it long, all the way down her back. She said she had some native

American blood, and judging from her high cheekbones and deep set eyes, that claim seemed plausible.

She owned a little ice cream shop in town where we would meet regularly to plot out how to attract crafters, where we would put them once they got here, and how to phrase their contacts to minimize confusion and complaints. In the ice cream shop I scoped out a long wall, free of decoration, and asked if I might display some small pictures that I had recently painted. These were simple little paint sketches of different details around the town and I figured it would help celebrate the bicentennial, as well as get the word around that I was doing art here. Lani very kindly agreed. We hung the paintings up and they looked good, definitely an improvement over the bare wall, at least.

Lani and I got along very well together, so when she mentioned that she needed part time help at the shop, I offered my services. That way I could babysit my art and make a few bucks at the same time.

Scooping ice cream is fairly pleasant work. People tend to be in good moods when they are out for a treat. Mostly I worked the early shift. Lani gave me a key to the shop so I could mop the floors and open the doors, while she got her husband and kids out the door on weekday mornings. Sometimes, if she had an emergency, I would take the afternoon shift, which meant closing up, counting out the till, and washing the spilled ice cream off the clear plastic tub lids, in a long trough sink in back. One afternoon, one of Lani's kids got off the bus in front of the shop and came in with magic marker drawings all over her face, arms and legs. Lani picked her up, dumped her into the trough sink and scrubbed off the marker ink, while the kid yelled her head off at the indignity of a fully clothed cold water bath. She made quite a racket. I was serving some customers up front while all the shouting was going on in back. The customers looked concerned. "We all scream for ice cream," I explained cheerfully.

Not many calamities befell us at the ice cream shop. We did have an extended power outage once, which resulted in 24 flavors of melted ice cream. Lani had to scramble to order more so that she could open the next day. I know that was an unexpected expense for her. The only other near disaster occurred when I came in the back door one morning and heard a great thrashing around up front.

Hoping that we weren't being robbed or something, I peeked around the doorway and found a starling flapping frantically about the shop. Evidence suggested that the bird had somehow fallen down the chimney, pecked it's way out through some drywall, and was now trapped in the shop. I opened the front doors and tried to scare the bird toward them, but it was too panicked to figure out how to escape. Gary, from the neighboring shop, came over to see what I was whooping and hollering at. He admitted to being petrified of birds and was no help at all, but watched the commotion from outside. Finally I found a tall glass cake dish top and trapped the poor thing between it and the front window. Gary was then able to get me a piece of cardboard, which I slid under the cake dish top. Once trapped, I carried the starling out the front door and let it go. The bird immediately blasted off for the next county. Bird poop was all over the shop, which I kept closed for two more hours so I could wipe everything down with bleach and plug the hole around the chimney. Needless to say, the bird never returned.

At a certain point I noticed a change in Lani. Maybe the ice cream business was not panning out as she had hoped, or maybe it was something else. She would ask me to stay an extra hour while she ran some errands, but then she would be gone for the whole rest of the day and, since we didn't yet have cell phones, I would be stuck there with no way to reach her. This happened with more frequency as time went on. Then came the reluctant paydays. I would ask for my paycheck and she would just sit there at her desk with her head in her hands. I asked her what was up (expecting that she was just broke) and she told me a story about how she had been in love a long time ago and they had broken up, but he had said he'd come back for her one day, and that she could feel him out there somewhere, trying to find her. It seemed like a storyline for a romance novel. I thought that maybe she was becoming depressed. But we had the craft fair to get through so I just hung on, hoping that things would improve as the weather got warmer.

One cool rainy day weekday morning I had opened the shop, but it was not an ice-cream eating sort of day. Gary from next door and another local lady were sitting around in the front room shooting the breeze. Gary was talking about watching college basketball on TV the previous night, when he suddenly glanced around himself with a twinkle in his eye and quipped that the guys on the court had looked like "a bunch of monkeys". I wasn't sure I had heard him right. "What do you mean by that?" I asked. He seemed surprised. "Well, you know, " he grinned and blushed, "they were all those downtown boys jumping around like monkeys." Obviously Gary had no idea that I all ready had some reputation for speaking up when I heard that sort of talk (or maybe he had heard, and was trying to see how far he could go before I blew up). "Gary," I barked, annoyed that I was again put in such a position, "Would you have said that if a black person was here in the store?" More smiling and blushing. "No," he muttered. "Well, don't say it in front of me, either," I told him. There was a long silence as I pretended to wipe down the counter. Finally the other local piped up. "You have to understand," she told me, "that this is just lil' old sleepy southern town." For a moment I was taken aback by her sudden Scarlet O'Hara impersonation. "Well, maybe it's time it woke up." I answered. Then I turned my back to them and pretended to re-stock the spoons and straws. When I turned around again, the two had disappeared back out into the rain.

I gave Lani notice of intent to leave her place of employment soon after that episode. There was no use staying on when I knew she was having trouble paying me and I had alienated some locals. She was fine with it, but asked if I could help out for a couple of hours during the bicentennial celebration. I agreed to do so, but since I had also agreed to help film the event, I told her that I couldn't stay past two o'clock when the parade began. She said that was fine.

The day of the bicentennial celebration went well. It was a fine, sunny day and the craft fair was running smoothly. Ice cream was selling well and Lani's older daughter came in to help, but wandered off after a while. Around noon Lani said she had to run out to check on things and I was left there to deal with crowds single-handedly. When two hours passed and Loni did not return, I had to put up the "Closed" sign and get out of there to film the parade, as promised. A few days later when I came by for my final paycheck, she was again reluctant to write it, but I busied myself by taking down my paintings from the wall and she finally got it together. That was the last time I saw her.

A few months later I noticed that the ice cream shop had closed. About a year after that I ran into Lani's husband and he told me that she had left him and the kids. I didn't ask where she had gone, but I wondered if that long lost love of hers had finally come back, or if she had simply had enough.

Chapter Eleven

LIBRARY CLERK

In a way, I blame a denim dress for my misadventures at the library. It had been given to me by a kindly neighbor who said it didn't fit her but would probably look good on me. It was a like-new shirt dress, pale blue, and rather out of fashion, but I accepted it graciously, not wanting to hurt my neighbor's feelings. It fit perfectly but was not at all my style. I figured it might come in handy if I was invited to a square dance, which is not out of the question when one lives in the country. I stuck it in my closet where it hung, unused for a long time. I had forgotten about it, until one day I found myself over-thinking what to wear to an interview for a clerk position at the local library. I wanted a dress that wasn't too fussy or too hippie-ish (like everything else in my closet) and there it was: that very sensible denim dress. That and a pair of sensible shoes and I looked every bit a library clerk.

I had spotted the part-time position of library clerk online and it sounded like just the thing for me. I like reading, and the library was walking distance from my house. I applied through the county government website, thinking at the time how fortunate I was that the job had opened up, since the local library branch had only been open for about a year at that time. My husband teased me for wanting to be a librarian, but in reality a librarian and a library clerk are two different things. A librarian is a person who has gone

through extensive training and has been certi-
fied to curate books and other resources for
the library. A library clerk is just a hired
schmo who enjoys books and wants to help
out.

I was interviewed by the head librarian
from the main branch, a sweet-faced younger
lady with long blonde hair whose looks did
not at all match her strict, no-nonsense personality. I guess that all that librarian training
and certification can do that to a person. She
was joined by the librarian of the branch at
which I hoped to work. This one was a skin-
ny, bespectacled, middle aged lady with a
severe, short haircut that exactly matched her
severe, short attitude. During the interview I
smiled and laughed and felt like a denim-clad
goofball. The two librarians were so tight-
lipped and stony-faced that I was not at all

confident that I would get the job. I was surprised when I was called in to work later that week.

The job itself was not difficult. Library clerks are expected to check books in and out, register library cards, check the book drop, answer the phone, and help people find books. They also keep the place in order by occasionally roaming around, scanning the shelves for books placed out of order, and replacing them according to their Boolean code numbers. This was manageable, except of course when people would leave their children unattended for long periods of time. The kids would often pull books off the shelf and leave them in heaps on the floor. This happened rather frequently. Luckily, our branch was small and there were only so many books in our children's department to toss into disarray.

I was a little disappointed to learn that although I was close enough to walk home, I was not allowed to leave the building during breaks. Lunch was to be eaten alone, in a little closet where all the discarded books were stored. That wasn't much fun. Also, since I was only a part-time employee of the county, I did not qualify for paid vacation time or other benefits. At least the salary was above minimum wage.

Still, the other people employed at the library were very nice and I liked them. There was another clerk besides me working there, and she and I got along quite well. She was a very quiet but intelligent, well-read person with a quick wit. We had lots of fun on Saturdays when the severe librarian had her day off. There were also some other wonderful people, who would come in and have regular story times with the children, which was entertaining for us because we got to see the little ones singing and having fun.

The severe librarian (whom I'll refer to as Vera) was much more of a challenge to my personality. She appeared to be trying to open up to me, but I had trouble relating to her. I like to find reasons to laugh, but she seemed to feel it was imperative to point out the deeply tragic edge in everything. For instance, if a bird was calling outside, she would *always* remark ruefully at how very, very sad it sounded. I got the feeling she was trying to impress everyone with how intensely sensitive she was. After a while her attitude grew tiresome. I guess she was depressed, but I've known a few depressed people in my life and at least they could make interesting conversation, sometimes. To me, Vera was just a perpetual downer. After a short while I found myself ducking away if I saw her approaching. More often than not I was stuck behind the circulation desk, unable to escape.

One evening, as we locked the library doors for the day, Vera asked if I could stay after closing time to hear some of her poetry. I really didn't want to. I was tired and wanted to go home, but because I wanted to be nice, and because I didn't know any better, I said that I could stay for just a couple of minutes. She began to read. Now, maybe it was because I had heard quite a bit of really fine poetry when I lived in downtown Washington D.C., or maybe it was because I could not quite relate to this lady, but I found nothing at all interesting or original about her work. Of course, I didn't say so, because she was my immediate supervisor. So after a few poems I just sort of nodded and said "Well, it's getting dark and I have to walk home..." but she didn't seem to get the hint. She pulled out another sheet of paper. "Just one more," she insisted, "This one is about a woman I once knew who meant a lot to me. I call it simply: 'Song'." The title alone made me feel as if my brain was crumbling like Feta cheese inside my cranium. Then came the realization that the words were describing the way some woman's body moved underneath her light summer dress. If I had been somewhat uncomfortable before, I was really uncomfortable, now. When she got to the end, she looked up at me expectantly. "Yeah, well, my husband will be home any minute so I really have to go," I said, and scuttled out the door like a threatened cockroach. "Oh crap," I muttered all the way home. I felt really bad for her, but she had crossed a line. "Oh crap." I knew my job was doomed.

I didn't mention this episode to anyone but my husband at the time. After that, things changed at the library. There were no more niceties between Vera and me. It was strictly business for a while, which was fine, but then she began to try to find fault. One afternoon I was talking with a regular visitor and Vera gave me a stern look and snapped "No chit-chatting!" I was taken aback. We had always conversed with library visitors before. As we were closing up that night she brought it up again. "I cannot tolerate chit-chat!," she said. "She was a neighbor," I explained, "I was only being friendly. Besides, you chat-chat to people all the time." Vera's face went red. "How dare you speak like that to your *superior*!" she hissed. I couldn't believe what I had just heard. *Superior?* Had I somehow wound up in some sort of drama about nuns? I fought to stifle a surprised laugh. Instead, I admitted to her that the job wasn't working out for me. I gave notice soon afterward.

My last two weeks as a library clerk were odd. There was a day when no-one else was scheduled to work but Vera and me. She did not show up. About a half hour after she was supposed to be there, I got a strange call on the phone. I think it was her, but I wasn't sure. The words were garbled and I couldn't make out what she was saying. Then she hung up. Mystified, I called the main branch and said that I thought that she had called in sick but wasn't sure, and that maybe someone there needed to call her back to verify. Nothing more was ever said about that incident.

After my last day as a library clerk, I walked home feeling both relieved and sorry. I was glad not to have to face Vera again, but I knew I would miss the other people there. As I walked along the town's old Main Street with my head held low, my mind was consumed with all I had been through, and I got the vague feeling I was making my way through a crowd of people. When I looked up I saw I was all alone on the street. It just so happened that it was Halloween, and I wondered if I had somehow walked through a party of ghosts. I almost felt like a ghost, myself. The Ghost of Library Clerks Past.

Some time later I was talking to a friend of the family, who was a retired head librarian. I told her that I had worked as a clerk, but had quit because I hadn't gotten along with the branch librarian. She asked me how old Vera had been. When I told her, she said, "I wonder if she was going through the change of life or something." She paused while a look of mild horror passed over her face. "Oh good lord, even I can't imagine having to work for a menopausal librarian." That made me feel a bit better.

I didn't set foot in that library branch until months later, after I had heard that Vera had left. I think she moved away. As for the sensible denim dress, I sent it off to the Goodwill. I hope it found its way to someone far more sensible than myself.

Chapter Twelve

FILMMAKING

When, after I had been a professional animated cartoon filmmaker for many years, I got a phone call asking if I would be available to ink and paint for an animation project, at first I didn't know what to say. It would be a huge step backward in my career, but they were paying Hollywood scale, which was as good as any real animator's pay I had ever seen on the east coast. The project was for new film technology company that had been started by a producer named Hugh, for whom I had worked as an animator previously. I was good friends with two of the people all ready hired for the project. Also, I had just taken on a mortgage with my husband on our first house and money was tight. So I said sure I'd help out, why not?

The company was very small. There were only four guys permanently employed there. One of them was a wonderful artist that I had worked with before, and he was the one who was animating the project. The only other temporary employee besides myself was Val, a vivacious red-headed woman, with whom I had worked previously as well.

Inking and painting animated cels is not too difficult, as long as one is consistent and persistent. Both Val and I had been haunting the downtown alternative music scene and liked the same sort of music, so it was rather relaxing to go in to work, put on the tunes, and ink and paint the day away, chatting as we worked. I caught up with Val, who told me all about her adventures as a filmmaker since last I had seen her. Though overqualified to be inking and painting, she too, was happy to have paying work between freelance projects.

Just after New Year's Day, a brand new calendar appeared in Hugh's office. It was one of those tool company calendars that featured oiled-up ladies in skimpy outfits leaning on cars while gazing lustfully at the camera. Since there was no other art on the wall behind his desk, the calendar looked for all the world like a comic strip thought balloon over Hugh's head. I would go in to talk to him, and it would appear that he was daydreaming about sweaty broads on cars the whole time. It was quite disconcerting.

Val and I both found the situation to be uncomfortable. We felt it was up to us to tact-
fully suggest the calendar's removal. We
summoned up our courage and presented our
case to Hugh. Hugh flatly refused to take it
down. He said it had been a present, and was
a collector's item. He even showed us the
caption on the cover, which read "Collector's
Item" (as if that would make any difference
to us). We made arguments. How were we
supposed to come in and talk seriously with
him when we had to face a photo of a greased
lady right behind him on the wall? Wouldn't
the calendar be more appropriate in a garage,
rather than in an executive office? What if a
visiting investor or client was a woman?
Could this lose her business?

Finally he got up and took the calendar off
the wall. Thank goodness he saw reason, we

thought. He then took the calendar down the hall to where the guys were eating lunch. Val and I followed and peeked in as Hugh held it up to the guys. "Is this offensive to you?" he asked them. Miserably, they stared at the floor and silently shook their heads. Triumphant, Hugh marched back to his office and hung the calendar back up on its thumbtack.

The next week, Hugh went out of town on a business trip. Dissatisfied with how our grievances had been disregarded, Val and I decided that we needed to 'decorate' the calendar as a protest. During our lunch breaks that week, we cut out pictures and captions from tabloids and pasted them onto the calendar. Now the greased ladies had dog heads, doll heads or baby heads, and captions such as "Best darned tomato I ever tasted". We laughed our heads off as we cut and pasted. We copied the pages on the xerox machine before returning the calendar to Hugh's office wall. Then we waited.

Remarkably, it took Hugh weeks to notice the difference, and each day Val and I laughed to ourselves in disbelief. Finally, it dawned on him that the calendar had been altered. He was not pleased. He threatened to make us pay for a new one, but we managed to peel the foreign material off and handed his precious calendar back to him. We did not, however, apologize. Irritably, he hung the calendar back up. A few weeks later it quietly disappeared. Val and I did not mention its absence, except to privately speculate that perhaps Hugh's wife had come in with their young daughter and had taken it down once and for all. Or maybe it had found a more permanent home in the men's restroom. At least Val and I didn't have to see it any more, and that was fine with us. I still have some photocopies of the 'decorated' version of that calendar, somewhere.

As the animation project drew to a close, Val was called to do another project on the west coast, and and took off. I remained and finished up the inking and painting. I had gotten used to a regular paycheck, so when Hugh asked if I could stay on as an employee, I considered it. The regular paycheck would be lower than what I had been making there as a freelancer, but it was money. Since I now lived in the boondocks and was somewhat removed from the downtown freelance loop, I decided to take the job.

Rather abruptly, things changed for me at work. Instead of being in the studio, I was moved to a desk in the lobby. Instead of working on projects, I was asked to answer phones and send letters. The terrible truth occurred to me that, after all my years of professional filmmaking, I had been given a receptionist job. Now, there is nothing wrong with being a receptionist if that's what you want to do, but I was bored out of my mind. Sure, I was getting paid for a lot of sitting around, but all I could think about was what I could be doing if I was home. I could be doing art. I could be reading. I could be writing. I could be gardening. It dawned on me that agreeing to stay on there had been a mistake.

I went to talk with Hugh, and he agreed to let me go, but he persuaded me to stay on just a bit longer to help with one more project.

That was great with me, as long as it didn't involve being a secretary. I was all done with that.

The project involved filming some hockey players, which Hugh imported temporarily from Canada. Why he didn't use U.S. hockey players, I don't know. The hockey players were flown down from Canada and spent the night in a hotel near the office. The next morning another fellow and I picked them up in a bus and drove them to an ice rink in Alexandria, some 30 miles away. I was relieved that the other fellow did the driving, since I was unfamiliar with Alexandria and had no idea where the ice rink was located.

The ice rink allowed us to film all night, during their regularly closed hours. So from 11pm to 6am we filmed the hockey players making goals and blocking shots. Some time during the night, the fellow who had driven the bus became ill, and had to be taken home. Since the other crew members had to pack up the equipment, I was left to take the hockey players back in the bus, myself. This was before electronic navigation was widely available and I wasn't sure what exit to take to get to the main highway home, but they assured me I would find it easily.

The hockey players boarded the bus. You might think they'd be exhausted after being up all night, like I was, but they weren't. They demanded that I stop at a bar so that they could get some beer. I told them that I was tired and wanted to get home, and that there were no bars that I knew of serving beer at 6am on a Sunday morning. They did not believe me. They were chanting "BEER!

BEER! BEER!" and having a grand old time, when I somehow missed the exit to head us back home. We were now lost on the beltway around Washington D.C. and seemed to be heading for Richmond. They found this hilarious. If I could have shriveled up and crawled under the dashboard I would have, but that would have greatly reduced our chances of making it back alive. As I fought my way toward anything that looked the least bit familiar, the boys became more obnoxious. They were making rude remarks about people outside the bus windows. Then they started heckling me. "Are you married?" they called to me from the back of the bus, "How many times a week do you have sex?" At that point they had stepped over the line. I wanted to slam on the brakes like a fed-up Dad on a road trip, but I kept driving. Finally I yelled back, "Look, I know some fascinating corners of Washington D.C., and I would be more than happy to just let you out and leave you there." They howled with laughter, but they backed off after that. Gradually they quieted down. By the time I found my way back to the highway and got us headed home I peeked at them in the rearview mirror. They had all fallen asleep. Thank God.

I had to awaken them when we got to their hotel. Bleary-eyed, they stumbled off the bus. The last guy off turned to me and said "I hope you don't think all Canadians are this rude." "I don't," I said, "Just the hockey players."

Needless to say, I was not the least bit sorry that that job was over.

As luck would have it, I was called by another friend soon afterward and wound up working as a freelance animator again. My faith in myself and in all humanity was once again restored.

* * *

My island of lost jobs is inhabited by other odd positions besides these. Don't get me started on the job I got painting out tiny dust spots on photographs. I think I lasted about two hours there. But in employment, as in life, sometimes we are faced with the decision of whether to go on with the show, or to just drop the ball. It's a juggling act. There really ought to be more circus music.

For the record, I forgive that last guy off the bus that day. I appreciate that he was trying to apologize. I don't actually think all Canadian Hockey players are rude. Just some of them. Likewise, I don't think all employers are rotten, just the ones who have proven themselves to be that way. To all the others, I am forever grateful.